To Emily,
   Never stop trying!
   Love Tigby a

Try like Tigby.

Spot the 🐟 on every page.

Tigby Tried

Meet Tigby,

a big red crab who loves adventures.

As much as Tigby loves adventures, they don't always go to plan.

Tigby
tried
baking,

EGGS

but he smashed the eggs.

Tigby tried knitting,

but he got tangled
in the wool.

Tigby

tried

gardening,

but he chopped the flowers off their stalks.

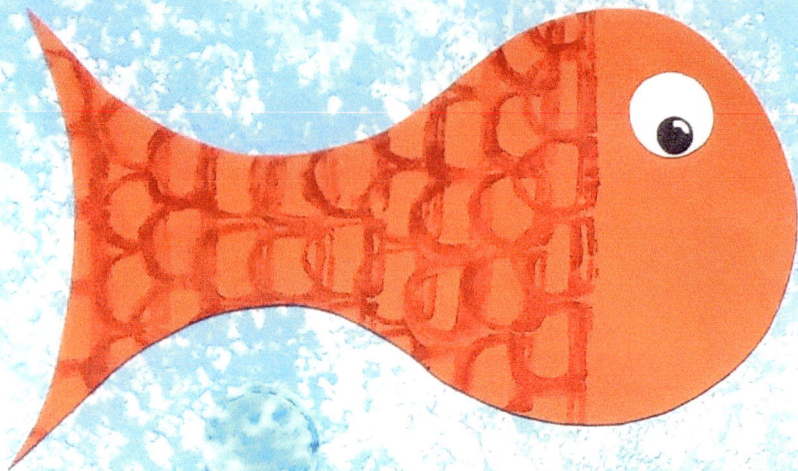

Tigby

tried

 fishing,

but he let the
fish slip away.

Tigby
tried
painting,

but he squirted himself with paint.

Tigby tried juggling,

but he dropped the beanbags on the floor.

Tigby tried skateboarding, but he wobbled off.

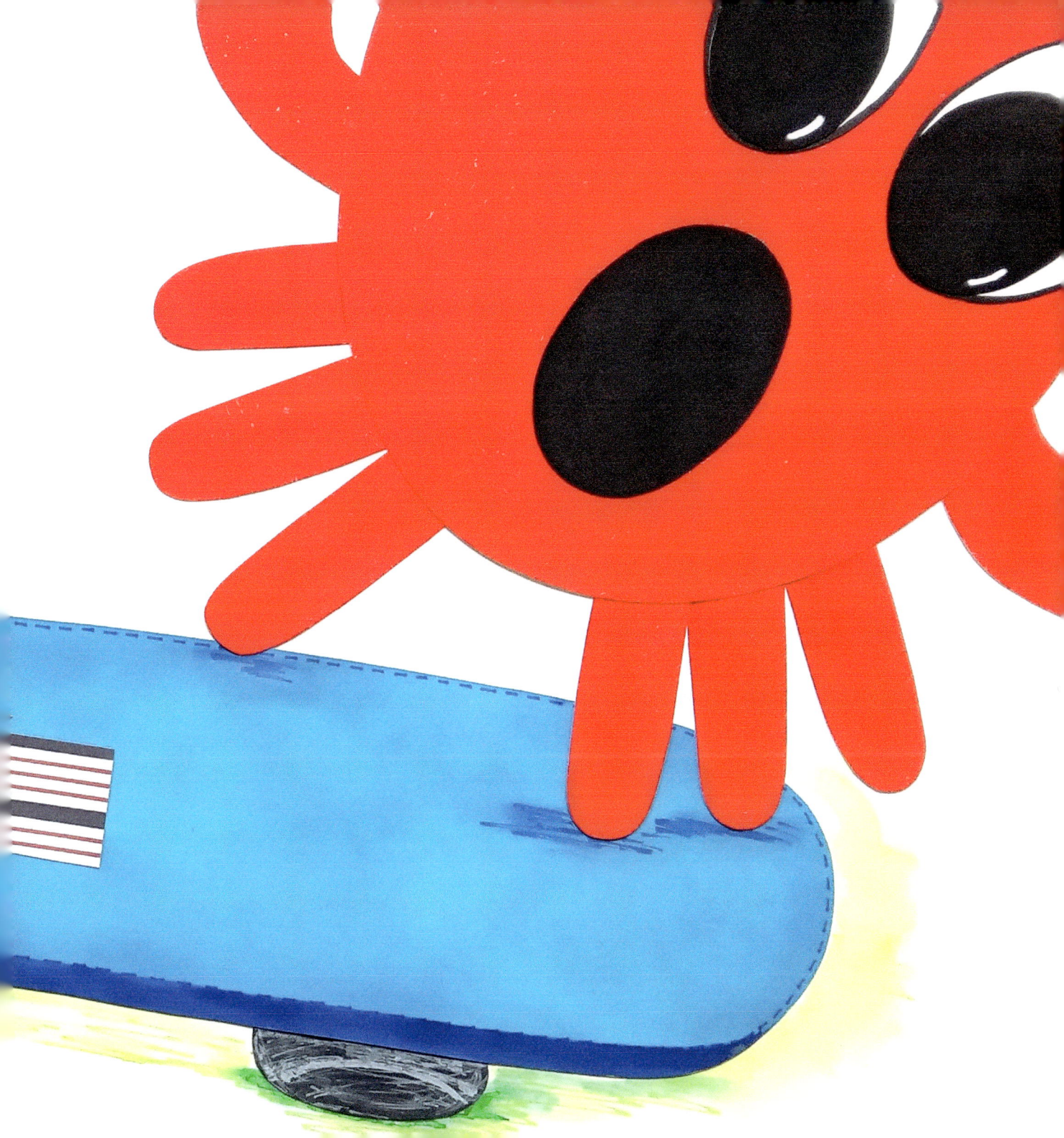

Tigby

tried

dancing,

but he got dizzy
spinning around.

Tigby tried ⭐ playing football,

but he tripped over
the ball.

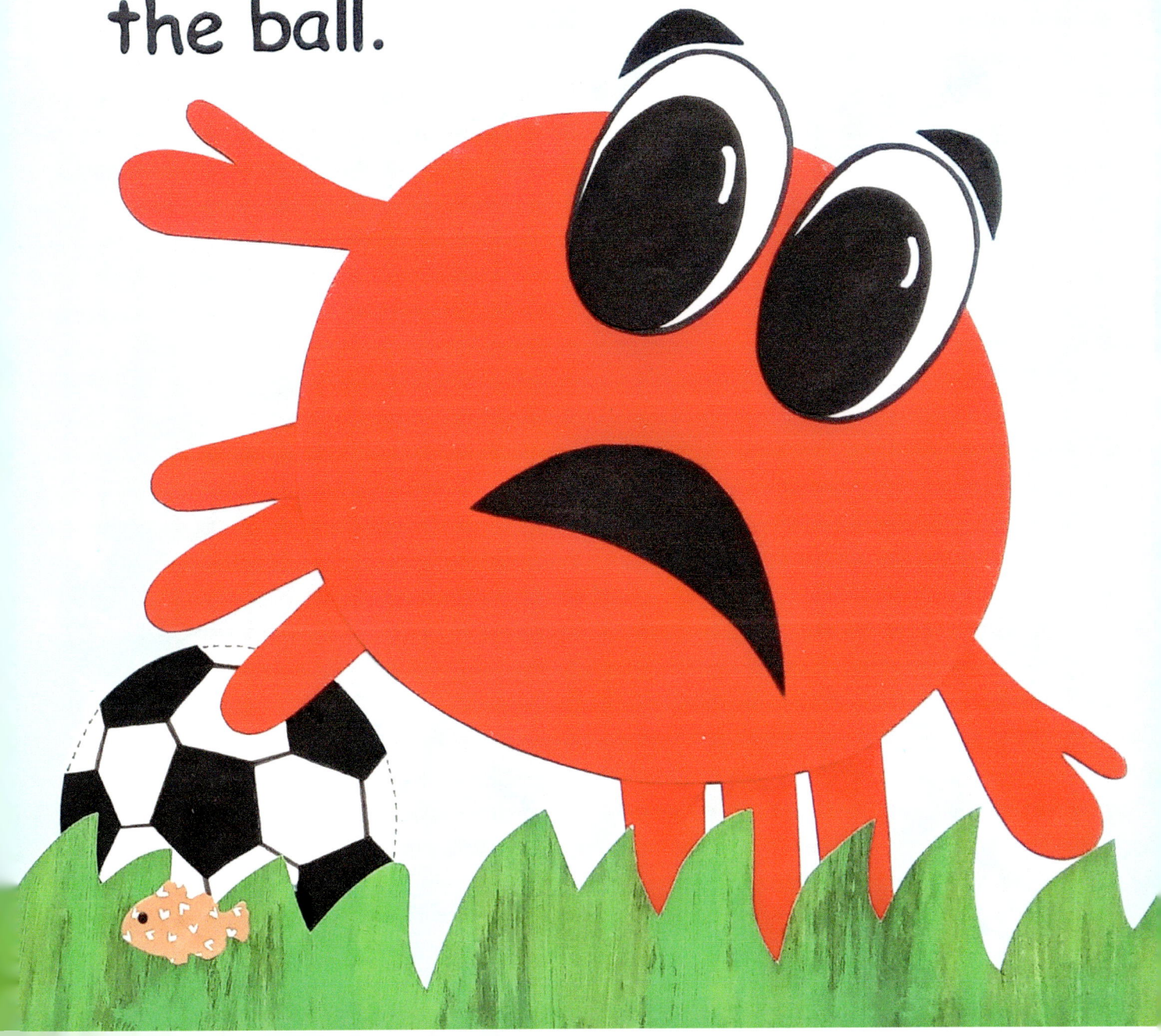

Tigby tried flying a kite,

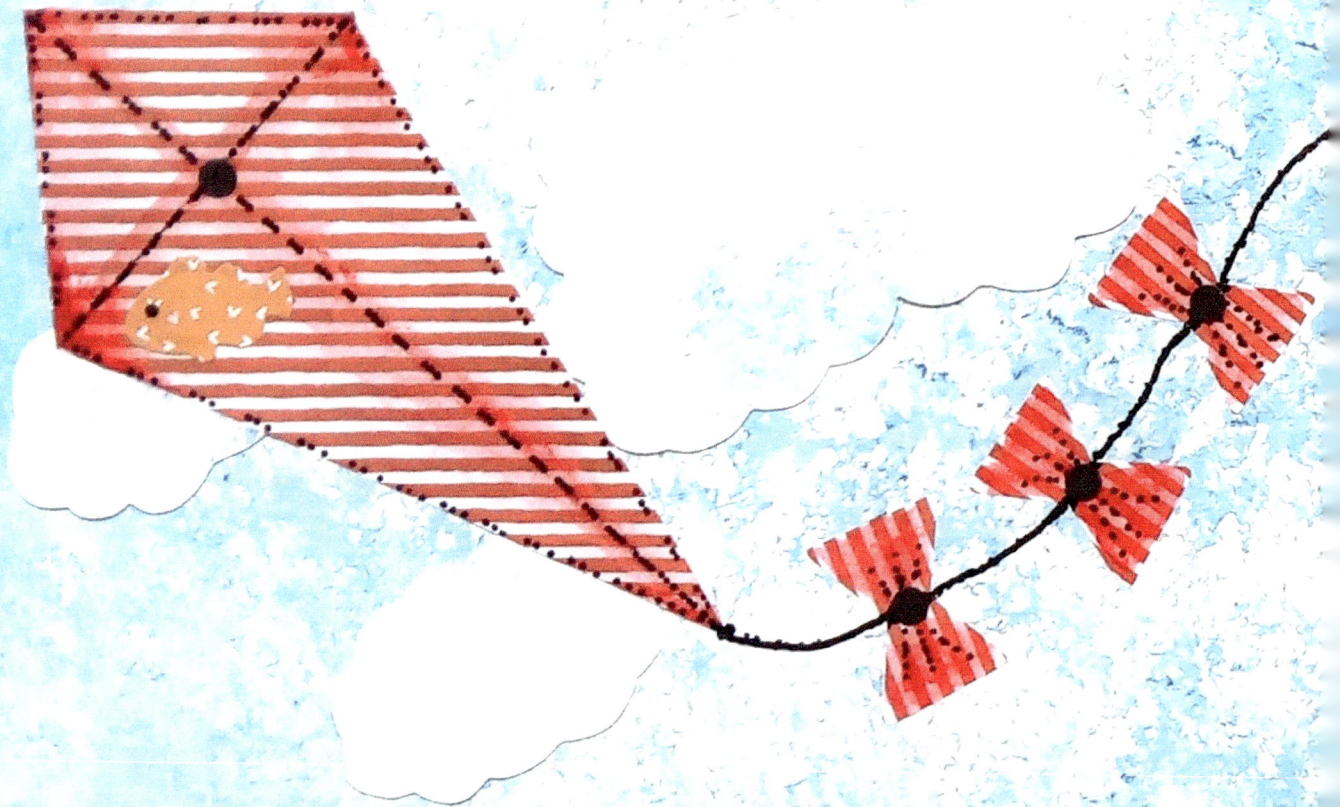

but he blew around in
the wind.

Tigby tried
Playing
hide and seek.

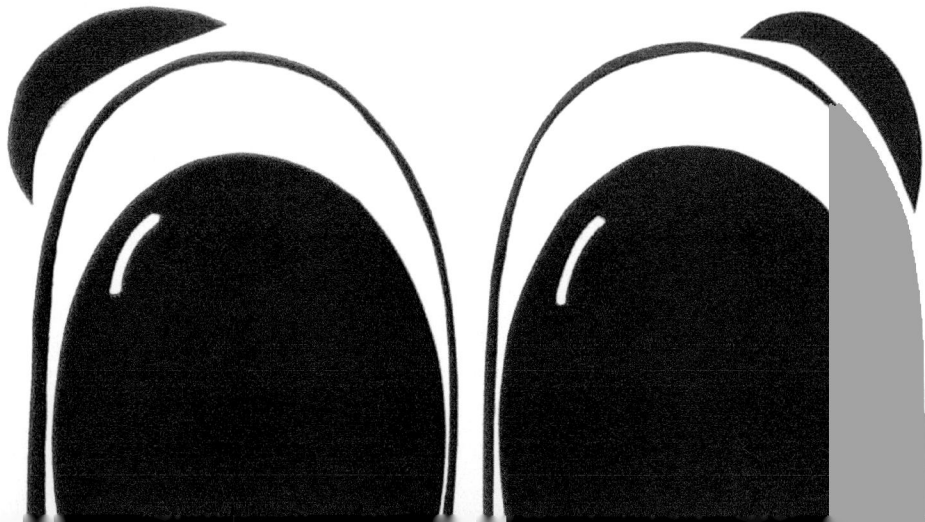

He LOVED it.